LOW FAT

[low fat UK]

© 1998 Rebo International b.v., The Netherlands
   1998 published by Rebo Productions Ltd.

Original recipes and photographs on pages 8-9, 10-11,
30-31,34-36,36-37,42-43,50-51,52-53,54-55,60-61,
62-63,64-65,66-67,70-71,74-75,78-79,88-89,92-93
© Ceres Verlag, Rudolf-August Oetker KG, Bielefeld, Germany

All other recipes and photographs © Quadrillion Publishing Ltd.,
Godalming, Surrey.

Design and creation by Consortium, England
Typeset by MATS, Southend-on-Sea, Essex
Edited by Anne Sheasby
Ceres Verlag recipes compiled and translated by Stephen Challacombe
Illustrations by Camilla Sopwith
Cover design by Minkowsky, buro voor grafische vormgeving,
Enkhuizen, The Netherlands

J0253UK

ISBN 1 84053 132 0

Printed in Slovenia

LOW FAT

SATISFYING AND FLAVOURSOME DISHES WITHOUT THE FAT

REBO
PRODUCTIONS

Contents

Introduction

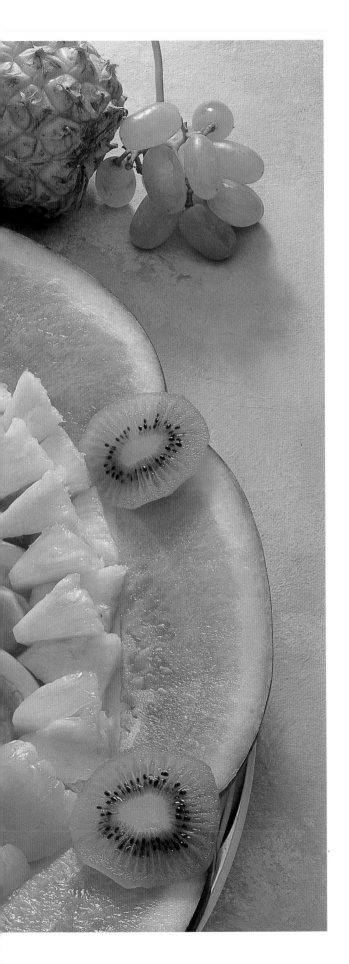

Most of us are now aware of one of the most prominent and important issues of healthy eating – that consuming too much fat in our daily diet is bad for us. A high-fat diet carries the risk of obesity and all the associated health problems because fatty foods are so loaded with calories. The key message to grasp is that it is the overall proportion of fats consumed in relation to our diet as a whole that matters, and the official recommendation is that fats should provide no more than 30-35% of our total calorie intake. But this, in fact, is only part of the story. It is actually certain kinds of fat that we should eat in limited amounts, namely saturated fats.

Saturated fats are naturally present in meat and dairy foods, and evidence suggests that when eaten to excess, these can increase blood cholesterol levels and with it the risk of coronary heart disease.

Just to confuse the issue, a certain amount of fat is vital for body function – it both provides and enables the body to absorb a variety of vitamins. Some fats are considered to be positively beneficial, such as fish oils found in sardines, herring, mackerel and salmon.

So what does all this boil down to in terms of what we should and should not eat from day to day? Liquid vegetable oils, such as olive, sunflower and safflower oils, are the healthiest choice for cooking and dressings as opposed to hard fats. Choose semi-skimmed or skimmed milk in preference to full-fat milk and low or half-fat varieties of other dairy products, such as cheese and yogurt. Use butter sparingly or a low-fat spread that is high in polyunsaturated fatty acids. Try to include at least two meals a week based on nuts or oily fish instead of meat. Always choose lean cuts of meat and trim off any visible fat. Grill or stew foods with little or no fat rather than frying or roasting them in added fat.

The recipes in this book have been specially selected for their low-fat and high nutritional content. But low fat need not mean low taste, as you will soon discover when you come to prepare and enjoy these delicious dishes. The mouth-watering aroma and flavour which fats impart to foods is provided instead by a wealth of fresh herbs, spices and seasonings to complement and enhance the taste of fresh, natural ingredients. So why not start right now and sample the sweet and savoury delights on offer in the following pages secure in the knowledge that you and your family will reap the benefits of healthy eating.

Pepper and Courgette Soup

A simple combination of fresh vegetables for a light and tasty soup.

Preparation time: 15 minutes • Cooking time: 30 minutes • Serves: 4

Ingredients

15 ml (1 tbsp) olive oil	5 ml (1 tsp) sea salt
1 large onion, thinly sliced	2.5 ml (½ tsp) ground black pepper
2 cloves garlic, thinly sliced or finely chopped	2.5 ml (½ tsp) ground paprika
700 ml (1¼ pints) vegetable stock	5 ml (1 tsp) cider vinegar
250 g (9 oz) courgettes, thinly sliced	1 sprig of fresh basil
200 g (7 oz) green pepper, seeded and chopped	Fresh basil sprigs, to garnish
250 g (9 oz) red pepper, seeded and chopped	

Method

1

Heat the oil in a pan, add the onion and cook until softened, stirring occasionally.

2

Add the garlic and cook gently for 5 minutes, stirring occasionally.

3

Add the stock, courgettes and peppers and stir to mix. Bring to the boil, cover and simmer for about 20 minutes, until the vegetables are tender, stirring occasionally.

4

Season the soup with the salt, pepper, paprika and cider vinegar.

5

Remove the leaves from the sprig of basil and chop just before serving the soup.

6

Ladle the soup into warmed soup bowls and serve, sprinkled with the chopped basil. Garnish with fresh basil sprigs.

Serving suggestions
Serve with fresh crusty bread or toast.

Variations
Use mushrooms in place of courgettes. Use 2 leeks in place of onion. Use fresh parsley or coriander in place of basil.

Marinated Peppers

This mixed pepper starter is always appealing with its vibrant colour and yielding texture.

Preparation time: 10 minutes, plus marinating time • Cooking time: 15 minutes • Serves: 4

Ingredients

1 red pepper	30 ml (2 tbsp) chopped fresh parsley
1 yellow pepper	Juice of ½ lemon
1 green pepper	30 ml (2 tbsp) olive oil
Salt and freshly ground black pepper	Fresh parsley sprigs, to garnish
2 cloves garlic	

Method

1

Place the peppers on a baking tray. Bake in a preheated oven at 250°C/475°/Gas Mark 9 for about 15 minutes, to blister the skins.

2

Remove from the oven and cover the peppers with a damp cloth. Set aside for 5 minutes.

3

Peel the peppers, then halve, core and seed. Cut into 3-cm (1¼-in) slices.

4

Lay the pepper slices on a platter and season with salt and pepper.

5

Peel and crush the garlic cloves and scatter over the peppers with the parsley.

6

Drizzle the lemon juice and oil over the peppers. Set aside to marinate for several hours before serving. Serve, garnished with fresh parsley sprigs.

Serving suggestions

Serve with crusty French bread or crispbreads.

Variations

Use lime juice in place of lemon juice. Use fat-free dressing in place of lemon juice and oil. Use walnut or hazelnut oil in place of olive oil.

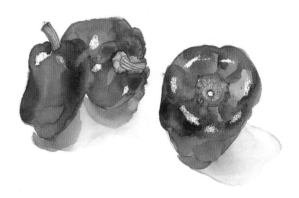

Carrot Soup

Carrots make a most delicious soup which is both filling and low in fat and calories.

Preparation time: 10 minutes • Cooking time: 30 minutes • Serves: 4

Ingredients

450 g (1 lb) carrots	2.5 ml (½ tsp) dried thyme
1 onion	2.5 ml (½ tsp) ground nutmeg
1 medium turnip	Salt and ground white pepper, to taste
2 cloves garlic, crushed	Toasted sunflower seeds, flaked almonds and pistachio nuts
700 ml (1¼ pints) water or vegetable stock	mixed together, to garnish

Method

1
Peel the carrots and cut into thick slices. Set aside.

2
Peel and roughly chop the onion and turnip.

3
Place the vegetables, garlic and water or stock in a large saucepan and bring to the boil. Cover the pan, reduce the heat and simmer for 20 minutes, stirring occasionally.

4
Stir in all the seasonings and simmer for a further 5 minutes.

5
Remove the soup from the heat and allow to cool slightly.

6
Purée the soup in a blender or food processor until it is thick and smooth.

7
Return to the rinsed-out pan and reheat the soup until piping hot, stirring occasionally.

8
Ladle into warmed soup bowls to serve and garnish with the sunflower seeds and mixed nuts.

Serving suggestion
Serve with fresh bread or bread rolls.

Orange, Grapefruit and Mint Salad

Fresh citrus fruits are complemented beautifully by the fragrant flavour of fresh mint.
Serve chilled for an ideal low-fat starter.

Preparation time: 20 minutes, plus chilling time • Serves: 4

Ingredients

2 grapefruit	*Liquid sweetener, to taste (optional)*
3 oranges	*8 sprigs of fresh mint*

Method

1
Using a serrated knife, cut away the peel and the white pith from the grapefruit and the oranges.

2
Carefully cut inside the skin of each segment to remove each section of flesh.

3
Squeeze the membranes over a bowl to extract all the juice. Sweeten the juice with the liquid sweetener, if using.

4
Arrange the orange and the grapefruit segments in an alternating pattern on 4 individual serving dishes.

5
Using a sharp knife, chop 4 sprigs of the mint very finely. Stir the chopped mint into the fruit juice.

6
Carefully spoon the juice over the arranged fruit segments and chill thoroughly before serving.

7
Serve each portion garnished with a fresh mint sprig.

Serving suggestions
Serve with a glass of freshly squeezed orange juice or oatcakes or crackers.

Variations
Use ruby or pink grapefruit and blood oranges when available in place of the normal types of fruit for a colourful variation.
Use borage leaves in place of the mint and garnish with a few of the blue flowers.

Cook's tips
Make sure all the white pith is removed from the fruit, since this produces a bitter flavour.
This dish can be prepared up to a day in advance and kept refrigerated.

Indian Tomato Soup

This highly aromatic and spicy tomato soup makes a lively low-fat starter.

Preparation time: 15 minutes • Cooking time: 20 minutes • Serves: 4

Ingredients

225 g (8 oz) tomatoes	15 ml (1 tbsp) tomato purée
1 onion	1 litre (1¾ pints) water or vegetable stock
15 ml (1 tbsp) olive oil	4-6 green curry leaves or 2.5 ml (½ tsp) curry powder
1 green chilli, seeded and finely chopped	Freshly ground sea salt, to taste
3 cloves garlic, crushed	Coriander leaves and green chillies, halved, to garnish

Method

1

Cut a small cross in the skin of each tomato and plunge into a bowl of boiling water for 30-40 seconds.

2

Remove the tomatoes and carefully peel away the loosened skin with a sharp knife.

3

Remove the hard cores from the tomatoes and roughly chop the flesh.

4

Peel the onion and chop into small pieces using a sharp knife.

5

Heat the oil in a large saucepan and gently cook the onion, chopped chilli and garlic for 3-4 minutes, until soft but not browned, stirring occasionally.

6

Stir in the chopped tomatoes and cook for 5 minutes, stirring frequently to prevent the vegetables from burning.

7

Blend the tomato purée with the water or stock and add to the pan. Add the curry leaves or powder and season with salt. Bring to the boil, then simmer for 5-7 minutes, stirring occasionally.

8

Remove the pan from the heat and stir in the coriander leaves and chilli halves.

9

Pour the soup into warmed serving bowls and serve piping hot, discarding the chilli garnish before eating.

Serving suggestion
Serve with wholemeal or mixed-grain bread.

Variation
Use yellow tomatoes for a change.

Cook's tips
Great care must be taken when preparing fresh chillies. Try not to get the juice into your eyes or mouth. If this should happen, rinse with lots of cold water. This soup freezes well, but should be frozen before adding the garnish.

Tomato and Pepper Ice

Similar to frozen gazpacho, this refreshing starter is ideal for serving on warm summer days.

Preparation time: 15 minutes, plus freezing time • Serves: 4-6

Ingredients

6 ice cubes	*5 ml (1 tsp) Worcestershire sauce*
125 ml (4 fl oz) canned tomato juice	*½ small green pepper, seeded and finely chopped*
Juice of 1 lemon	*½ small red pepper, seeded and finely chopped*

Method

1
Break the ice into small pieces using a small hammer.

2
Place the broken ice into a blender or food processor with the tomato juice, lemon juice and Worcestershire sauce.
Blend the mixture until it becomes slushy.

3
Pour the tomato mixture into ice trays or a shallow freezerproof container and freeze for ½ hour,
or until it is just half frozen.

4
Remove the tomato ice from the freezer trays and place in a bowl.

5
Mash the tomato ice with the back of a fork until the crystals are thoroughly broken up.

6
Mix in the peppers and return the tomato ice to the freezer trays.

7
Re-freeze for a further 1½ hours, stirring occasionally to prevent the mixture from solidifying completely.

8
To serve, allow the tomato ice to defrost for about 5 minutes, then mash with the back of a fork to
roughly break up the ice crystals. Serve in small glass dishes which have been chilled beforehand.

Serving suggestion
Scoop out tomatoes and serve the tomato ice in the shells instead of glass dishes.

Variations
Use lime juice in place of lemon juice. Use chilli sauce in place of Worcestershire sauce.

Cook's tips
Take care not to allow the tomato ice to freeze into a solid block, or it will be too hard to break into the rough crystals.
This recipe will freeze for up to 2 months.

Salmon Paté

This highly nutritious, elegant paté is low in fat and very quick to prepare.

Preparation time: 15 minutes • Serves: 4

Ingredients

225 g (8 oz) canned red or pink salmon, drained	*1.25 ml (¼ tsp) Tabasco sauce*
140 g (5 oz) low-fat curd cheese	*Freshly ground sea salt and black pepper, to taste*
A few drops of lemon juice	*30 ml (2 tbsp) 0%-fat fromage frais or low-fat plain yogurt*
A pinch of ground mace or ground nutmeg	*4 small gherkins*

Method

1

Remove and discard any bones and skin from the salmon. In a bowl, work the fish
into a smooth paste with the back of a spoon.

2

In a separate bowl, beat the curd cheese until it is smooth.

3

Add the salmon, lemon juice, seasonings and fromage frais or yogurt and mix well until thoroughly incorporated.

4

Divide the mixture equally between 4 individual ramekins. Smooth the surfaces evenly.

5

Slice each gherkin lengthways 4 or 5 times, making sure that you do not cut completely
through the gherkin at the narrow end.

6

Splay the cut ends into a fan and use these to decorate the tops of the patés in the ramekins. Serve.

Serving suggestions

Serve with wholemeal toast, melba toast or crispy wholemeal rolls.

Variations

Use canned tuna fish in place of the salmon and stir in 5 ml (1 tsp) horseradish sauce in place of the
Tabasco sauce. Use cottage cheese in place of curd cheese.

Cook's tip

If you have a blender or food processor, you can work the curd cheese and salmon together
in this instead of beating them in a bowl.

Lamb and Noodle Soup

A hearty soup based on lamb stock with mushrooms and lean cooked lamb.

Preparation time: 15 minutes • Cooking time: 30 minutes • Serves: 4

Ingredients

115 g (4 oz) transparent noodles	*175 g (6 oz) lean cooked lamb, thinly sliced*
6 dried Chinese mushrooms, soaked for 15 minutes in warm water and drained	*15 ml (1 tbsp) soy sauce*
	A few drops of chilli sauce
700 ml (1½ pints) lamb stock, skimmed	*Salt and freshly ground black pepper*

Method

1

Break the transparent noodles into small pieces and cook in a saucepan of lightly salted, boiling water
for 20 seconds. Rinse in fresh water and set aside to drain.

2

Cook the mushrooms in a saucepan of lightly salted, boiling water for 15 minutes,
rinse in fresh water and set aside to drain.

3

Cut the mushrooms into thin slices.

4

Heat the stock in a saucepan and add the mushrooms, lamb, soy sauce and chilli sauce.
Season with salt and pepper.

5

Bring to the boil, then reduce the heat and simmer gently for 15 minutes, stirring occasionally.

6

Stir in the drained noodles and simmer just long enough for the noodles to heat through. Serve immediately.

Serving suggestion

Serve with soft fresh bread or bread rolls.

Variations

Use fresh Chinese noodles in place of the transparent noodles. Use lean beef and beef stock in place of lamb.

Cook's tip

If the noodles are too hard to break with your fingers, use a serrated knife to cut them.

Vegetable Kebabs

A colourful and flavoursome way to serve delicious fresh vegetables as part of a low-fat diet.

Preparation time: 30 minutes, plus standing and marinating time • Cooking time: 10 minutes • Serves: 4

Ingredients

1 large aubergine	12-14 button mushrooms
Salt	30 ml (2 tbsp) olive oil
1 large green pepper	30 ml (2 tbsp) lemon juice
4 courgettes	2.5 ml (½ tsp) salt
12-14 cherry tomatoes, red or yellow	2.5 ml (½ tsp) freshly ground black pepper
12-14 pickling onions	Fresh parsley sprigs, to garnish

Method

1
Cut the aubergine in half and cut into 2.5-cm (1-in) pieces.

2
Place the aubergine pieces in a large bowl and sprinkle liberally with salt. Stir well, then allow to stand for 30 minutes.

3
Rinse the aubergine pieces thoroughly in a colander under cold water to remove all traces of salt. Drain well.

4
Cut the pepper in half. Remove and discard the core and seeds. Cut the pepper flesh into 2.5-cm (1-in) pieces with a sharp knife.

5
Slice the courgettes diagonally into pieces about 2.5-cm (1-in) thick.

6
Remove the tough cores from the cherry tomatoes and peel the onions. Rinse the mushrooms
under cold water to remove any soil, but do not peel.

7
Place all the prepared vegetables in a large bowl and add the remaining ingredients. Mix well to coat evenly,
cover with plastic wrap and allow to stand for about 30 minutes, stirring the vegetables once or twice
to ensure they remain evenly coated.

8
Thread the vegetables alternately on to skewers and arrange on a grill pan.

9
Brush the kebabs with the marinade and grill for 3-5 minutes, turning frequently and basting with the marinade
until they are evenly browned. Serve piping hot, garnished with fresh parsley sprigs.

Serving suggestion
Serve with a mixed leaf salad and fresh crusty bread.

Variations
Use any combination of your favourite vegetables in this recipe. Use lime juice or orange juice in place of lemon juice.

Cook's tip
Salting the aubergines removes any bitter juices and some of the vegetable's moisture.

Aubergine Bake

Aubergines are filling vegetables, and are especially delicious when baked in the oven.

Preparation time: 30 minutes, plus marinating time • Cooking time: 20-30 minutes • Serves: 6

Ingredients

2 large or 3 medium-sized aubergines	*2.5 ml (½ tsp) chilli powder*
10 ml (2 tsp) salt	*5 ml (1 tsp) crushed garlic*
150 ml (¼ pint) malt vinegar	*2.5 ml (½ tsp) ground turmeric*
15 ml (1 tbsp) olive oil	*8 tomatoes, sliced*
2 large onions, sliced into rings	*300 ml (½ pint) low-fat plain yogurt*
2 green chillies, seeded and finely chopped	*5 ml (1 tsp) freshly ground black pepper*
425-g (15-oz) can peeled plum tomatoes, chopped	*85 g (3 oz) half-fat Cheddar cheese, finely grated*

Method

1

Cut the aubergines into 5-mm (¼-in) thick slices. Arrange the slices in a shallow dish and sprinkle with 5 ml (1 tsp) of the salt. Pour over the malt vinegar, cover the dish and marinate for 30 minutes.

2

Drain the aubergines well, discarding the marinade liquid.

3

Heat the oil in a frying pan and gently fry the onion rings until they are golden brown.

4

Add the chillies, the remaining salt, chopped tomatoes, chilli powder, garlic and turmeric. Mix well and simmer for 5-7 minutes until thick and well blended, stirring occasionally.

5

Remove the sauce from the heat and cool slightly. Blend to a smooth purée using a blender or food processor.

6

Arrange half the aubergine slices in the base of a lightly greased shallow ovenproof dish.

7

Spoon half the tomato sauce over the aubergine slices. Cover the tomato sauce with the remaining aubergine, then top with the remaining tomato sauce and sliced tomatoes.

8

Mix together the yogurt, black pepper and cheese. Pour evenly over the tomato slices.

9

Bake in a preheated oven at 190°C/375°F/Gas Mark 5 for 20-30 minutes, or until the topping bubbles and turns golden brown. Serve hot straight from the oven.

Serving suggestion

Serve with cooked fresh vegetables such as broccoli florets and carrots and boiled new potatoes.

Variations

Use red onions in place of standard onions. Use half-fat Red Leicester cheese in place of Cheddar.

Cook's tip

Make sure that the aubergines are well drained when they are removed from the marinade. Press them into a colander using the back of your hand to remove all excess vinegar. Do not rinse since the vinegar gives a delicious tangy flavour to the dish.

Okra Casserole

Okra has an interesting texture and a mild flavour which combines well with tomatoes to make this delicious Mediterranean-style casserole.

Preparation time: 15 minutes • Cooking time: 20 minutes • Serves: 4

Ingredients

15 ml (1 tbsp) olive oil	*Juice of ½ lemon*
1 small onion, sliced	*Salt and freshly ground black pepper*
225 g (8 oz) okra	*30 ml (2 tbsp) chopped fresh parsley*
6 ripe tomatoes	

Method

1
Heat the oil in a large saucepan, add the onion and cook until soft and transparent but not browned, stirring occasionally.

2
Remove just the stems from the okra but leave on the pointed tail. Take care not to cut off the very top of the okra.

3
Add the okra to the onions and cook gently for 10 minutes, stirring occasionally.

4
Meanwhile, cut a small cross in the skins of the tomatoes and plunge into a bowl of boiling water for 30 seconds.

5
Drain the tomatoes and carefully peel away and discard the loosened skins. Chop the peeled tomatoes roughly.

6
Add the tomatoes, lemon juice, seasoning and parsley to the okra and continue to cook for about a further 5 minutes, or until the tomatoes are just heated through, stirring occasionally.

7
Spoon into a serving dish and serve hot or cold.

Serving suggestion
Serve with oven-baked potatoes topped with a little low-fat spread or reduced-fat cheese.

Variations
Use green beans in place of okra. Use fresh coriander or basil in place of parsley.

Cook's tips
If you cannot find fresh okra, use canned okra in its place, but drain and rinse before use and reduce the cooking time by half. If too much liquid is left at the end of cooking, remove the vegetables with a slotted spoon and boil the liquid quickly to reduce the sauce.

Tomato Flan

A satisfying fresh tomato and red pepper flan with a crispy breadcrumb topping.

Preparation time: 25 minutes • Cooking time: 20 minutes • Serves: 4-6

Ingredients

700 ml (1¼ pints) vegetable stock	*5 ml (1 tsp) paprika*
150 g (5½ oz) semolina	*2.5 ml (½ tsp) chopped fresh or dried marjoram*
30 ml (2 tbsp) olive oil	*300g (10½ oz) quark (low-fat curd cheese)*
2 red peppers, seeded and thinly sliced	*1 kg (2 lb 4 oz) beefsteak tomatoes, sliced*
1 onion, sliced	*40 g (1½ oz) wholemeal breadcrumbs*
1 leek, sliced	*Fresh herb sprigs, to garnish*
1 clove garlic, finely chopped	

Method

1

Bring the stock to the boil in a saucepan, add the semolina and cook for about 15 minutes, stirring occasionally. Remove from the heat and set aside.

2

Heat 15 ml (1 tbsp) of the oil in a pan and lightly cook the red peppers, onion, leek and garlic until softened, stirring occasionally.

3

Season with paprika and marjoram and cook for a further 10 minutes, stirring occasionally.

4

Stir the quark into the cooked semolina.

5

Grease a glazed earthenware flan dish and spread the mixture over the dish. Lay the tomato slices over the semolina.

6

Sprinkle with the breadcrumbs and drizzle over the remaining oil.

7

Bake in a preheated oven at 230°C/450°F/Gas Mark 8 for about 20 minutes, until cooked and golden brown. Serve, garnished with fresh herb sprigs.

Serving suggestion

Serve with a mixed green salad and crusty French bread.

Variations

Use yellow peppers in place of red peppers. Use oregano in place of marjoram.

Dolmas

Delicious individual parcels of rice, herbs, nuts and fruit make a very different and tasty low-fat lunch or supper dish.

Preparation time: 30 minutes • Cooking time: 30-40 minutes • Serves: 6

Ingredients

12 large cabbage leaves, washed	*55 g (2 oz) currants*
175 g (6 oz) long-grain rice	*Salt and freshly ground black pepper*
8 spring onions	*Juice of 1 lemon*
15 ml (1 tbsp) chopped fresh basil	*30 ml (2 tbsp) olive oil*
15 ml (1 tbsp) chopped fresh mint	*150 ml (¼ pint) low-fat plain yogurt*
15 ml (1 tbsp) chopped fresh parsley	*115 g (4 oz) cucumber*
55 g (2 oz) pine nuts	

Method

1
Using a sharp knife, trim away and discard any tough stems from the cabbage leaves.

2
Place the leaves in a saucepan of boiling water for about 30 seconds. Remove using a slotted spoon and drain thoroughly before laying out flat on a work surface.

3
Place the rice in a saucepan along with enough boiling water to just cover. Cook for 15-20 minutes, or until the rice is soft and the liquid is almost completely absorbed. Rinse the rice in cold water to remove any starchiness. Drain well.

4
Cut the spring onions into thin diagonal slices. Place the rice and the onions in a large bowl with the remaining ingredients, except 15 ml (1 tbsp) of the oil, yogurt and cucumber. Mix the rice mixture thoroughly to blend evenly.

5
Place about 30 ml (2 tbsp) of the rice filling on each blanched cabbage leaf, pressing it gently into a sausage shape.

6
Fold the sides of the leaves over to partially cover the stuffing, then roll up, Swiss-roll style, to completely envelop the filling.

7
Place the rolls seam side down in a large baking dish and brush with the remaining oil. Pour hot water around the cabbage leaves until it comes about halfway up their sides.

8
Cover the baking dish with aluminium foil, pressing it gently onto the surface of the leaves to keep them in place. Bake in a preheated oven at 190°C/375°F/Gas Mark 5 for 30-40 minutes.

9
Meanwhile, peel the cucumber and cut it lengthways into quarters. Remove the seeds and discard. Chop the cucumber flesh and half of the peel into very small pieces.

10
In a bowl, mix together the cucumber and yogurt, cover and chill until required.

11
Drain the dolmas from the cooking liquid and arrange on a serving plate with a little of the cucumber sauce spooned over. Serve.

Serving suggestions
Serve the dolmas either hot or cold with oven-baked potatoes or pitta bread.

Variations
Use vine leaves in place of cabbage leaves. Use lime juice in place of lemon juice.

Cook's tip
Dolmas can be prepared a day in advance and allowed to stand in their liquid in the refrigerator.

Stuffed Pumpkin

In this attractive dish, a pumpkin is filled with a delicious mixture of cheese, rice and fruit, then baked in the oven until tender.

Preparation time: 35 minutes, plus 1 hour standing time • Cooking time: 1½-2 hours • Serves: 4-6

Ingredients

1 soft-skinned pumpkin, weighing about 3 kg (6 lb 8 oz)	1 yellow pepper
45 ml (3 tbsp) soy sauce, plus extra to taste	15 ml (1 tbsp) butter
30 ml (2 tbsp) lemon juice	200 g (7 oz) long-grain rice
15 ml (1 tbsp) Worcestershire sauce	500 ml (18 fl oz) vegetable stock
5 ml (1 tsp) honey	1 small fresh pineapple, weighing about 750 g (1 lb 10 oz)
2 cloves garlic, crushed	175 g (6 oz) half-fat Mozzarella, cut into small pieces
Freshly ground black pepper	6 spring onions, sliced into rings
1 red pepper	115 g (4 oz) beansprouts
1 green pepper	2.5 ml (½ tsp) finely grated lemon rind

Method

1
Slice off the top of the pumpkin and remove and discard the seeds and fibres.

2
In a small bowl, mix together the 45 ml (3 tbsp) soy sauce, lemon juice, Worcestershire sauce and honey.

3
Add 1 crushed clove garlic to the mixture and season with pepper.

4
Rub the mixture over the inside of the pumpkin and set aside for 1 hour.

5
Cut the peppers in half, remove and discard the cores and seeds and cut into small chunks.

6
Melt the butter in a pan, add the peppers and rice and cook for 5-10 minutes. Stir in the vegetable stock.

7
Bring to the boil, then reduce the heat and simmer for about 15 minutes, stirring occasionally.

8
Meanwhile, peel the pineapple, cut into quarters, then remove and discard the core. Chop the flesh into cubes.

9
Add the cheese, pineapple, spring onions, beansprouts, lemon rind and the remaining garlic to the rice and pepper mixture. Season with pepper and soy sauce and stir well to mix.

10
Place the rice mixture in the pumpkin, replace the top and place in a baking dish.

11
Bake in a preheated oven at 180°C/350°F/Gas Mark 4 for 1½-2 hours, or until the pumpkin is cooked and tender. Once the pumpkin skin blisters, add a little water to the dish from time to time. Serve.

Serving suggestion
Serve with a vegetable ribbon salad.

Variations
Use a marrow in place of the pumpkin. Use fresh mango or peaches in place of pineapple.
Use half-fat Cheddar cheese in place of Mozzarella.

Three-Bean Hot Salad

A quick and easy yet satisfying salad combining black-eye beans, red kidney beans and butter beans.

Preparation time: 15 minutes • Cooking time: 15 minutes • Serves: 4-6

Ingredients

125 ml (4 fl oz) sherry vinegar	225 g (8 oz) canned, drained red kidney beans
90 ml (6 tbsp) olive oil	225 g (8 oz) canned, drained butter beans
3 cloves garlic	10 black olives, stoned
1 bay leaf	2 red onions, sliced
2.5 ml (½ tsp) each dried basil, oregano and tarragon	1 bunch radishes, thinly sliced
2.5 ml (½ tsp) salt	2 pickled green chillies, seeded and sliced
Freshly ground black pepper	Fresh herb sprigs, to garnish
225 g (8 oz) canned, drained black-eye beans	

Method

1

In a bowl, whisk together 125 ml (4 fl oz) water, the sherry vinegar and oil. Pour into a saucepan.

2

Add 2 cloves of garlic to the liquid, together with the bay leaf, dried basil, oregano and tarragon, salt and a little black pepper. Stir well, then bring to the boil.

3

Add the beans and simmer for 10 minutes, stirring occasionally. Remove from the heat.
Remove and discard the garlic and bay leaf.

4

Slice the olives into strips and thinly slice the remaining clove of garlic. Add to the bean mixture with the onions, radishes and chillies. Mix well.

5

Adjust the seasoning with salt and pepper and serve slightly warm, garnished with fresh herb sprigs.

Serving suggestion

Serve with fresh crusty bread or bread rolls.

Variations

Use a mixture of canned beans of your choice. Use cider vinegar in place of sherry vinegar.
Use standard onions in place of red onions.

Chinese Cabbage with Smoked Meat

A delectable combination of Chinese cabbage, citrus fruits and smoked meat,
tossed together in a light mayonnaise dressing.

Preparation time: 15 minutes • Serves: 4

Ingredients

350 g (12 oz) Chinese cabbage	*45 ml (3 tbsp) reduced-fat/calorie mayonnaise*
200 g (7 oz) smoked lean meat, such as chicken or ham	*150 ml (¼ pint) low-fat plain yogurt*
3 oranges	*15 ml (1 tbsp) Cognac*
1 grapefruit	*Salt and freshly ground black pepper*
125 g (4½ oz) black grapes	

Method

1

Remove the stalk of the cabbage, shred the leaves, then wash and drain. Place in a bowl and set aside.

2

Slice the smoked meat into thin strips. Add to the cabbage and toss to mix.

3

Peel the oranges and grapefruit, segment the fruit and squeeze out and reserve the juice. Add to the cabbage and mix.

4

Cut the grapes in half and remove and discard the seeds. Add to the cabbage and toss to mix.

5

For the dressing, place the juice from the citrus fruit in a small bowl with the mayonnaise, yogurt,
Cognac and salt and pepper to taste and mix thoroughly.

6

Pour or spoon the dressing over the salad and toss to mix thoroughly.

7

Serve immediately or cover and chill before serving.

Serving suggestions

Serve with crusty French bread or toast, or oven-baked potatoes with a little grated reduced-fat cheese.

Variations

Use white, green or red cabbage in place of Chinese cabbage. Use unsmoked lean meat such as turkey, chicken
or beef in place of the smoked meat. Use pink or ruby grapefruit for a change.

Salade Paysanne

This homely salad can be made with any selection of fresh vegetables you have to hand.

Preparation time: 20 minutes • Serves: 6

Ingredients

4 spring onions	2 sprigs fresh coriander or chopped fresh parsley
½ cucumber	2.5 ml (½ tsp) salt
3 carrots	2.5 ml (½ tsp) freshly ground black pepper
6 large tomatoes	15 ml (1 tbsp) cider vinegar
10 button mushrooms	15 ml (1 tbsp) apple juice
3 sticks celery	30 ml (2 tbsp) olive oil
1 green pepper, cored, seeded and chopped	A pinch of mustard powder
15-20 tiny cauliflower florets	Liquid sweetener, to taste (optional)
15-20 radishes, quartered	8 lettuce leaves, to garnish
15 ml (1 tbsp) chopped watercress or mustard and cress	

Method

1
Trim the spring onions and slice diagonally into thin slices.

2
Peel the cucumber and quarter lengthways. Use a sharp knife to remove the soft, seedy centre and discard. Dice the flesh.

3
Peel the carrots and thinly slice diagonally.

4
Cut a small cross in the skins of each tomato, then plunge into a bowl of boiling water for 30 seconds. Remove the tomatoes and carefully peel away and discard the blanched skin. Quarter the peeled tomatoes and remove the tough cores.

5
Thinly slice the mushrooms and sticks of celery.

6
Place all the prepared vegetables in a bowl with the coriander and parsley and mix well.

7
For the dressing, mix together all the remaining ingredients, except the lettuce leaves. Whisk thoroughly using a fork or balloon whisk, until the mixture becomes thick and cloudy.

8
Arrange the lettuce leaves on a serving dish and pile the prepared mixed vegetables on top.

9
Just before serving, spoon a little of the dressing over the salad and serve the remainder separately in a small jug. Serve immediately.

Serving suggestions
Serve with reduced-fat cheese or lean chicken for a light lunch or snack.

Variations
Use lemon juice in place of apple juice. Use walnut or hazelnut oil in place of olive oil.

Pan-Fried Salad

This flavourful salad offers a medley of fresh vegetables, fruits and nuts mixed with rice
and tossed in a piquant dressing.

Preparation time: 10 minutes • Serves: 2-4

Ingredients

100 g (3½ oz) long-grain rice	*50 g (1¾ oz) sultanas*
Salt and freshly ground black pepper	*30 ml (2 tbsp) cider vinegar*
Paprika, to taste	*45 ml (3 tbsp) apple juice*
Corn kernels from 2 cooked corn cobs	*1 clove garlic, thinly sliced*
175 g (6 oz) mung beans	*1 spring onion, chopped*
25 g (1 oz) flaked almonds	*55 g (2 oz) radicchio, shredded*
15 ml (1 tbsp) sesame oil	

Method

1

Place the rice in a saucepan. Add 250 ml (9 fl oz) water and salt and pepper and paprika to taste. Stir to mix.

2

Bring to the boil, then reduce the heat. Cover and simmer for about 30 minutes, or until the rice is
cooked and tender. Remove the pan from the heat.

3

Add the corn, mung beans and almonds to the rice and mix well.

4

Heat the oil in a frying pan, add the rice and corn mixture and stir-fry for about 5 minutes, until piping hot.

5

Remove the pan from the heat and add the sultanas, vinegar, apple juice, garlic, spring onion and radicchio.

6

Toss thoroughly to mix well. Adjust the seasoning and serve warm or cold.

Serving suggestions

Serve with crusty fresh bread or cooked fresh vegetables such as baby carrots and courgettes.

Variations

Use orange or pineapple juice in place of apple juice. Use raisins or chopped ready-to-eat apricots or
peaches in place of sultanas. Use chopped hazelnuts in place of almonds.

Black Olive and Cauliflower Salad

The exciting flavours of the Mediterranean combine in this recipe to produce a refreshingly different salad.

Preparation time: 20 minutes • Cooking time: 20 minutes, plus chilling time • Serves: 4

Ingredients

15 ml (1 tbsp) olive oil	*45 ml (3 tbsp) tomato purée*
1 large cauliflower, broken into florets	*115 g (4 oz) black olives, stoned*
1 large Spanish onion, sliced	*Salt and freshly ground black pepper*
Juice of ½ lemon	*30 ml (2 tbsp) chopped fresh parsley*

Method

1
Heat the oil in a large sauté or frying pan and gently cook the cauliflower for 2 minutes, stirring occasionally. Remove the cauliflower to a plate and set aside.

2
Add the onion to the pan and cook for 2 minutes, until softened, stirring occasionally.

3
Return the cauliflower to the pan and add 150 ml (¼ pint) water and the lemon juice. Bring to the boil, reduce the heat and simmer until tender, adding a little more water if the mixture begins to boil dry, stirring occasionally.

4
Using a slotted spoon, remove the cauliflower from the pan, reserving the juices. Place the cauliflower on a plate and set aside.

5
Add the tomato purée to the liquid in the pan, stir to mix, then boil rapidly to reduce.

6
Stir the chopped olives into the juices in the pan and heat through. Season to taste with salt and pepper.

7
Arrange the cauliflower florets on a serving dish and spoon the olive sauce over the top. Cool, then chill well before serving.

8
Sprinkle with the chopped parsley just before serving.

Serving suggestion
Serve with warm ciabatta or country-style bread.

Variations
Use green olives instead of black. Use broccoli in place of cauliflower. Use sesame oil in place of olive oil.

Cook's tip
To remove the stones from olives, roll the olives firmly on a flat surface with the palm of your hand to loosen the stones. Remove the stones using a cherry stoner or the tip of a potato peeler.

Stir-Fried Vegetable and Tofu Salad

This filling vegetarian salad is full of interesting texture.

Preparation time: 25 minutes, plus chilling time • Cooking time: 3 minutes • Serves: 4-6

Ingredients

250 g (9 oz) tofu	45 ml (3 tbsp) lemon juice
115 g (4 oz) mangetout	10 ml (2 tsp) honey
55 g (2 oz) mushrooms	5 ml (1 tsp) grated fresh root ginger
2 carrots	45 ml (3 tbsp) soy sauce
2 sticks celery	A dash of sesame oil
4 spring onions	25 g (1 oz) unsalted roasted peanuts
60 ml (4 tbsp) olive oil	115 g (4 oz) beansprouts
55 g (2 oz) broccoli florets	½ head Chinese leaves

Method

1
Drain the tofu well and press gently to remove any excess moisture. Cut into 1-cm (½-in) cubes. Set aside.

2
Trim the tops and tails from the mangetout. Thinly slice the mushrooms with a sharp knife.

3
Cut the carrots and celery diagonally into thin slices.

4
Trim the spring onions and slice diagonally. Set aside.

5
Heat 15 ml (1 tbsp) of the olive oil in a wok or large frying pan. Add the mangetout, mushrooms, carrots, celery and broccoli and stir-fry for 2 minutes.

6
Remove the vegetables from the wok and set aside on a plate or in a bowl to cool.

7
Place the remaining olive oil in a small bowl and whisk in the lemon juice, honey, ginger, soy sauce and sesame oil.

8
Stir the spring onions, peanuts and beansprouts into the cooled vegetables.

9
Mix the dressing into the salad vegetables, then add the tofu. Toss the tofu into the salad very carefully so that it does not break up.

10
Shred the Chinese leaves and arrange on a serving platter. Pile the vegetables and tofu over the top and serve well chilled.

Serving suggestions
Serve with oven-baked potatoes or crusty fresh bread rolls.

Variations
Use shredded cooked lean chicken or beef in place of tofu for a non-vegetarian option. Use sugar-snap peas in place of mangetout. Use garlic in place of ginger. Use walnuts in place of peanuts.

Cook's tip
Make sure that the stir-fried vegetables are completely cool before adding the remaining salad ingredients, or they will lose their crispness.

Orange Baked Herring

Quick to prepare, this dish uses the tangy taste of orange to offset the richness of the herring.

Preparation time: 10 minutes • Cooking time: 6-8 minutes (microwave on HIGH) • Serves: 4

Ingredients

4 herrings, gutted and cleaned	*15 ml (1 tbsp) chopped fresh dill*
4 bay leaves	*25 g (1 oz) butter, softened*
Juice and finely grated rind of ½ orange	*Orange slices, to garnish*

Method

1

Rinse the fish and dry well. Place a bay leaf inside each fish. Place each fish on a sheet of non-stick baking parchment.

2

In a bowl, beat the orange juice, rind and dill into the butter. Divide the butter into 4 and spread some over each of the fish.

3

Wrap each parcel separately, making sure the fish is totally enclosed.

4

Cook in a microwave oven on HIGH for 6-8 minutes, until the fish is cooked, turning the fish parcels halfway through the cooking time.

5

Serve in the paper, garnished with orange slices. Remove and discard the bay leaves before serving.

Serving suggestion

Serve with freshly cooked French beans and almonds, or mangetout.

Variations

Use other herbs such as tarragon or chives in place of dill. Use lemon rind and juice in place of orange. Use small trout in place of herrings.

Cook's tip

If preferred, or if the fish are large, the heads and tails of the fish can be removed before or after cooking.

Rice Salad with Prawns

A luxurious seafood rice dish for an appetising lunch or supper.

Preparation time: 15 minutes, plus standing time • Cooking time: 20 minutes • Serves: 2

Ingredients

150 g (5½ oz) long-grain rice	30 ml (2 tbsp) lemon juice
1 large eating apple	A little grated fresh root ginger
Lime juice, to sprinkle	Salt
3 fresh pineapple rings	Cayenne pepper
30 ml (2 tbsp) reduced-calorie mayonnaise	A pinch of sugar
30 ml (2 tbsp) half-fat crème fraîche	150 g (5½ oz) cooked, peeled prawns
15-30 ml (1-2 tbsp) curry powder	15 ml (1 tbsp) sunflower seeds

Method

1

Cook the rice in a large saucepan of lightly salted, boiling water for about 20 minutes, until cooked and tender.

2

Drain, rinse under cold water and drain again thoroughly. Set aside to cool.

3

Peel, core and slice the apple and sprinkle with a little lime juice. Cut the pineapple into small chunks. Set aside.

4

For the dressing, in a bowl, mix the mayonnaise with the crème fraîche, curry powder, lemon juice and ginger.

5

Season to taste with salt and cayenne pepper and add the sugar.

6

Place the rice, apple and pineapple in a bowl, add the dressing and toss to mix well.
Cover and set aside for 30 minutes to allow the flavours to mingle.

7

Before serving, stir in the prawns. Heat the sunflower seeds in a frying pan for a few minutes,
then sprinkle over the salad to serve.

Serving suggestion

Serve with crusty fresh bread or bread rolls and a pepper, onion and tomato salad.

Variations

Use 1-2 eating pears in place of the apple. Use canned, flaked tuna or salmon or cooked crab meat in place of prawns.

Oven-Baked Fish Cutlets with Tomatoes

A trouble-free and delicious way of serving fish with the minimum of fat.

Preparation time: 10 minutes, plus 30 minutes standing time • Cooking time: 25 minutes • Serves: 4

Ingredients

4 firm white fish cutlets such as cod or halibut, each weighing about 200 g (7 oz)	*A sprig of fresh basil*
	4 small knobs of butter
Juice of 1 lemon	*Fresh basil sprigs, to garnish*
6 tomatoes	

Method

1
Place the fish in a baking dish, sprinkle with lemon juice and set aside for 30 minutes.

2
Quarter the tomatoes and remove and discard the cores. Finely chop the basil.

3
Place the tomatoes over the fish and sprinkle over the basil.

4
Top each piece of fish with a knob of butter and cover with foil.

5
Bake in a preheated oven at 200°C/400°F/Gas Mark 6 for about 25 minutes, or until the fish is cooked and the flesh is just beginning to flake.

6
Serve, garnished with fresh basil sprigs.

Serving suggestion
Serve with boiled new potatoes, mangetout and carrots.

Variations
Use lime or orange juice in place of lemon juice. Use plum tomatoes for a change.

Cook's tip
Each individual cutlet can be wrapped and sealed in a foil parcel with the other ingredients, placed on a baking tray and baked as above. Unwrap the parcels and serve opened on a plate.

Fish Fillets with Garden Cress Purée

In this unusual dish, fish fillet rolls are filled with a tasty potato and cress purée, then oven-baked.

Preparation time: 30 minutes • Cooking time: 20 minutes • Serves: 4-6

Ingredients

600 g (1 lb 5 oz) skinless white fish fillets such as sole or plaice	1 egg yolk
	2 punnets of garden cress
30 ml (2 tbsp) lemon juice	1 egg white
Salt and freshly ground black pepper	5 ml (1 tsp) butter
250 g (9 oz) potatoes, diced	Fresh herb sprigs, to garnish
45 ml (3 tbsp) half-fat crème fraîche	

Method

1

Cut the fish into strips about 4-5 cm (1½-2 in) wide and sprinkle with lemon juice and season with salt. Set aside.

2

Cook the potatoes in a saucepan of boling water for 10-15 minutes, until tender.

3

Drain thoroughly, cool slightly, then purée in a blender or food processor until smooth. Place in a bowl.

4

Add the crème fraîche and egg yolk to the potato purée and mix well.

5

Wash the cress, cut off the roots and stir into the potato mixture. Season with salt and pepper.

6

Beat the egg white until stiff, then fold into the potato mixture.

7

Grease a shallow ovenproof dish with the butter. Spread the potato purée over the fish fillets, loosely roll up and place in the prepared dish.

8

Cover with foil and bake in a preheated oven at 200°C/400°F/Gas Mark 6 for about 20 minutes, or until the fish is cooked and the flesh is just beginning to flake. Serve, garnished with fresh herb sprigs.

Serving suggestion

Serve with minted new potatoes, broccoli florets and green beans.

Variations

Use chopped watercress in place of garden cress. Use sweet potatoes in place of standard potatoes.

Sole Kebabs

These kebabs are ideal for cooking out of doors on a barbecue for a low-fat summer treat.

Preparation time: 20 minutes, plus marinating time • Cooking time: 8 minutes • Serves: 4

Ingredients

8 skinless fillets of sole	*Salt and freshly ground black pepper*
30 ml (2 tbsp) olive oil	*3 drops of Tabasco sauce or pepper sauce*
1 clove garlic, crushed	*3 medium courgettes*
Juice of ½ lemon	*1 green pepper*
Finely grated rind of ½ lemon	*Chopped fresh parsley, to garnish*

Method

1
Cut each sole fillet in half lengthways and roll up each slice Swiss-roll style.

2
Mix together the oil, garlic, lemon juice, rind and seasonings in a small bowl.

3
Place the rolls of fish in a shallow, non-metallic dish and pour over the lemon and oil marinade.
Cover the dish and allow to stand in a cool place for at least 2 hours.

4
Cut the courgettes into 5-mm (¼-in) slices. Cut the pepper in half lengthways and remove and
discard the core and seeds. Cut the pepper flesh into 2.5-cm (1-in) squares.

5
Carefully thread the marinated sole fillets onto kebab skewers, alternating with pieces of the prepared vegetables.
Brush each kebab with a little of the oil and lemon marinade.

6
Arrange the kebabs on a grill pan and cook under a moderately hot grill for about 8 minutes, turning frequently
to prevent burning and brushing with the extra marinade to keep moist during cooking.

7
Arrange the kebabs on a serving dish and sprinkle with chopped parsley to garnish. Serve hot.

Serving suggestion
Serve with stir-fried fresh mixed vegetables and oven-baked potatoes.

Variations
Use plaice in place of sole. Use lime rind and juice in place of lemon. Use red or yellow pepper in place of green pepper.

Cook's tip
After 2 hours marinating, the sole will look opaque and have a partially cooked appearance.

Paprika Schnitzel

Thin slices of fillet of pork are served with a rich-tasting paprika sauce for a delicious low-fat meal.

Preparation time: 20 minutes, plus chilling time • Cooking time: 20 minutes • Serves: 4

Ingredients

8 thin slices of fillet of pork, cut along the fillet	*1 green pepper, seeded and cored*
Salt and freshly ground black pepper	*15 ml (1 tbsp) paprika*
1 clove garlic, crushed	*150 ml (¼ pint) beef stock*
15 ml (1 tbsp) olive oil	*125 ml (4 fl oz) red wine*
1 onion, sliced	*45 ml (3 tbsp) tomato purée*
1 red pepper, seeded and cored	*150 ml (¼ pint) low-fat plain yogurt*

Method

1
Trim the slices of pork to remove any fat and flatten with a rolling pin until 5-mm (¼-in) thick.

2
Rub both sides of the pork slices with salt, pepper and garlic, then place on a plate and refrigerate for 30 minutes.

3
Heat the oil in a large frying pan and cook the pork fillets in several batches if necessary, until they are well browned and cooked right through. This will take about 4 minutes on each side.

4
Remove the pork from the pan and place on a plate. Cover, set aside and keep warm.

5
Add the onion and peppers to the oil and meat juices in the frying pan and cook quickly for about 3-4 minutes, until soft but not browned, stirring occasionally.

6
Add the paprika, stock, wine and tomato purée to the frying pan and bring the mixture to the boil.

7
Reduce the heat and simmer until some of the liquid has evaporated and the sauce has thickened. Season with salt and pepper to taste.

8
Arrange the pork slices on a serving dish and pour the paprika sauce over the top.

9
Beat the yogurt in a bowl until smooth. Carefully drizzle over the paprika sauce to make an attractive pattern. Swirl gently into the sauce to blend, but take care not incorporate it completely. Serve hot.

Serving suggestion
Serve with mashed potatoes, mangetout and cauliflower.

Variations
Use lean beef fillet in place of pork. Use white wine or apple juice in place of stock.

Cook's tips
If the yogurt is too thick to drizzle properly, whisk in a little water or skimmed milk to thin to the required consistency. This dish freezes well for up to 3 months.

Curly Endive with Marinated Turkey

A delicious warm salad of tender turkey and crisp mixed leaves – ideal for a special lunch or supper.

Preparation time: 15 minutes, plus 30 minutes marinating time • Cooking time: 10-15 minutes • Serves: 2-4

Ingredients

200 g (7 oz) skinless, boneless turkey breast fillet	125 ml (4 fl oz) double cream
125 ml (4 fl oz) dry sherry	Wine vinegar, to taste
5 ml (1 tsp) honey	Salt, to taste
5 ml (1 tsp) redcurrant jelly	1 head of curly endive
5 ml (1 tsp) curry powder	1 head of radicchio
5 ml (1 tsp) ground paprika	1 small avocado
A pinch of ground ginger	15 ml (1 tbsp) olive oil
Freshly ground white pepper	100 g (3½ oz) mushrooms, sliced
15 ml (1 tbsp) butter	5 salted whole almonds

Method

1
Slice the turkey into thin strips and set aside.

2
To prepare the marinade, in a bowl, mix together the sherry, honey, redcurrant jelly, curry powder, paprika, ginger and pepper.

3
Add the turkey and mix well to coat all over. Set aside to marinate in a cool place for 30 minutes.

4
Using a slotted spoon, remove the turkey from the marinade and place on a plate. Reserve the marinade.

5
Melt the butter in a frying pan, add the turkey and cook until golden brown all over and
cooked through, turning occasionally. Set aside.

6
Add the marinade to the pan and stir in the cream. Bring to the boil and cook for about 3 minutes over a high heat. Add the
vinegar and salt to taste. Remove from the heat and keep warm.

7
If necessary, tear large leaves of curly endive and radicchio into smaller pieces. Halve the avocado,
remove the stone and discard. Peel, then cut into slices. Set aside.

8
Heat the oil in a pan, add the mushrooms and cook briefly. Keep warm.

9
Dry-fry the almonds in a frying pan until lightly browned.

10
Place all the vegetables on a dish, arrange the turkey on top, then serve the lukewarm sauce separately.
Serve immediately, garnished with the almonds.

Serving suggestion
Serve with warm ciabatta or country-style bread.

Variations
Use chicken in place of turkey. Use apple juice or red or white wine in place of sherry. Use chilli powder in place of curry powder.
Use courgettes in place of mushrooms.

Ragout of Lamb with Okra

A heart-warming casserole of lean, succulent lamb, onions, tomatoes and fresh okra.

Preparation time: 15 minutes • Cooking time: 1½-2 hours • Serves: 4-6

Ingredients

1.5 kg (3 lb 5 oz) lean leg of lamb	*700 ml (1¼ pints) meat stock*
4 beefsteak tomatoes	*250 g (9 oz) okra, trimmed*
15 ml (1 tbsp) olive oil	*2 cloves garlic, crushed*
2 onions, sliced	*Salt and freshly ground black pepper*
1 bunch of fresh parsley, finely chopped	*Fresh herb sprigs, to garnish*

Method

1
Slice the lamb into pieces about 4-cm (1½-in) wide. Cut the tomatoes into 8 pieces, discarding the tough cores.

2
Heat the oil in a pan, add the lamb and cook until browned all over.

3
Add the onions and tomatoes and cook for a further 10 minutes, stirring occasionally.

4
Sprinkle the parsley over the lamb mixture, then add the stock. Bring to the boil, cover, then reduce the heat and simmer for 1-1½ hours, or until the lamb is cooked and tender, stirring occasionally.

5
Add the okra and garlic to the pan and stir to mix. Allow the okra to cook for 10-15 minutes, or until tender. Season with salt and pepper before serving. Serve, garnished with fresh herb sprigs.

Serving suggestion
Serve with boiled rice and a mixed leaf salad.

Variations
Use lean beef or pork in place of lamb. Use leeks in place of onions. Use baby courgettes or green beans in place of okra.

Chicken and Vegetable Pilaf

This simple rice dish, cooked in the microwave for convenience, is full of flavour yet low in fat.

Preparation time: 15 minutes • Cooking time: 25 minutes (microwave) • Serves: 4

Ingredients

500 g (1 lb 2 oz) skinless, boneless chicken breasts	*225 g (8 oz) prepared mixed soup vegetables, such as turnip, swede, carrots and parsnips or peas*
15 ml (1 tbsp) butter	*2 leeks, washed*
15 ml (1 tbsp) ground paprika	*125 g (4½ oz) mushrooms, sliced*
Salt and freshly ground black pepper	*4 tomatoes, skinned and sliced*
150 g (5½ oz) long-grain rice	*15-30 ml (1-2 tbsp) chopped fresh parsley*
250 ml (9 fl oz) chicken or vegetable stock	
2 onions, chopped	

Method

1
Preheat a large browning dish in a microwave oven on HIGH for about 7 minutes.

2
Meanwhile, flatten the chicken with a rolling pin, then slice into 4-cm (1½-in) cubes.

3
Place the butter in the browning dish to melt. Add the chicken, press down slightly,
then cook, uncovered, on HIGH for 1 minute.

4
Turn and cook on HIGH for a further 1 minute. Season with the paprika and salt and pepper to taste.

5
Add the rice and stock to the dish and cover. Cook on HIGH for 6 minutes, stirring once halfway through the cooking time.

6
Add all the vegetables to the rice and chicken, mix together well and season with salt and pepper.
Cover and cook on HIGH for 3 minutes.

7
Stir the mixture, cover, then cook on MEDIUM for a further 1 minute, stirring once or twice.

8
Remove from the oven and leave the covered dish at room temperature for about 10 minutes before serving.
Season if required, sprinkle with chopped parsley and serve.

Serving suggestion
Serve with crusty French bread.

Variations
Use lean turkey, beef or pork in place of chicken. Use fresh coriander in place of parsley.

Warm Rabbit Salad

Pan-fried rabbit is tossed together with marinated vegetables in this tasty dish.

Preparation time: 15 minutes, plus marinating time • Cooking time: 20 minutes • Serves: 2-4

Ingredients

100 g (3½ oz) green beans, trimmed	1 bunch of radishes, sliced
15 ml (1 tbsp) wine vinegar	150 g (5½ oz) mushrooms, sliced
30 ml (2 tbsp) walnut oil	2 skinless rabbit quarters
Salt and freshly ground pepper	15 g (½ oz) butter
1 red pepper, seeded, cored and cut into strips	Fresh basil sprigs and black peppercorns, to garnish
1 green pepper, seeded, cored and cut into strips	

Method

1

Blanch the beans in a saucepan of boiling water for 1 minute, then plunge into a bowl of ice-cold water.
Drain, place in a bowl and set aside.

2

Place the wine vinegar and oil in a bowl, season with salt and pepper and whisk thoroughly to mix.

3

Add the peppers, radishes and mushrooms to the beans. Drizzle over the dressing and set aside to marinate for 15 minutes.

4

Meanwhile, rub salt and pepper into the rabbit quarters. Melt the butter in a frying pan and fry the
rabbit evenly on both sides for about 20 minutes, or until cooked through.

5

Remove the rabbit from the pan and thinly slice, discarding any bones. Add to the vegetable salad.

6

Divide the salad between 2-4 plates. Sprinkle each plate of salad with fresh basil sprigs and peppercorns and serve.

Serving suggestions
Serve with oven-baked potatoes or fresh bread.

Variations
Use chicken or turkey in place of rabbit. Use mangetout in place of green beans. Use wild mushrooms for a change.

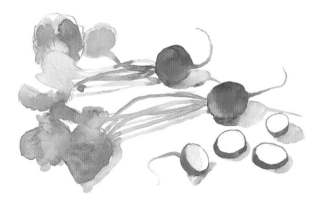

Turkey and Sage Kebabs

Fresh sage lends fragrant flavour to low-fat turkey in this appealing dish.

Preparation time: 20 minutes, plus marinating overnight • Cooking time: 30 minutes • Serves: 6

Ingredients

1.25 kg (2 lb 12 oz) skinless turkey meat	*Salt and freshly ground black pepper, to taste*
10 ml (2 tsp) chopped fresh sage	*115 g (4 oz) lean back bacon, rind and fat removed and discarded*
1 sprig of fresh rosemary, chopped	
Juice of 1 lemon	*Whole sage leaves*
15 ml (1 tbsp) olive oil	*Fresh sage leaves, to garnish*

Method

1

Remove and discard any bone from the turkey and cut the meat into evenly sized cubes.

2

Place the chopped sage, rosemary, lemon juice, oil and salt and pepper in a large bowl and stir in the turkey, mixing well to coat evenly. Cover and leave in the refrigerator overnight.

3

Cut the bacon strips in half lengthways, then again crossways.

4

Wrap the bacon around as many of the cubes of marinated turkey as possible.

5

Thread the turkey and bacon rolls alternately with the sage leaves and any unwrapped turkey cubes onto kebab skewers.

6

Place the kebabs on a grill rack in a grill pan and grill under a preheated moderate grill for about 30 minutes, turning frequently and basting with the marinade while cooking. Serve immediately, garnished with fresh sage leaves.

Serving suggestions

Serve with pitta bread and salad or on a bed of cooked rice.

Variations

Use chicken or lean pork in place of turkey. Use lime or orange juice in place of lemon.
Use lean smoked back bacon for a change.

Cucumber Cocktail

This refreshing drink makes an excellent summer aperitif.

Preparation time: 10 minutes • Serves: 4-6

Ingredients

2-3 cucumbers, weighing about 1 kg (2 lb 4 oz)	*Caster sugar*
Lemon juice	*Celery salt*
Salt and freshly ground black pepper	*Finely chopped fresh mint, to garnish*

Method

1

Peel the cucumbers and cut in half lengthways. Scrape out and discard the seeds.

2

Cut the cucumbers into pieces and purée in a blender or food processor until smooth.

3

Transfer to a bowl or jug and stir in lemon juice, salt and pepper, sugar and celery salt to taste.

4

Pour into glasses, garnish with a little chopped mint and serve immediately or cover and chill before serving.

Serving suggestion

Serve with a light starter such as a fish paté.

Variations

Use garlic salt in place of celery salt. Use lime juice in place of lemon juice.
Use skinned, seeded tomatoes in place of cucumber.

Tropical Fruit Health Drink

This low-fat healthy fruit drink makes an ideal breakfast-time treat.

Preparation time: 10 minutes • Serves: 4

Ingredients

3 kiwi fruit	*1 lime*
2 ripe nectarines or peaches	*300 ml (½ pint) unsweetened pineapple juice*
2 slices fresh pineapple	*1 kiwi fruit or lime, sliced, for decoration*

Method

1

Carefully remove the peel from the kiwi fruit and roughly chop the flesh. Set aside.

2

Plunge the nectarines or peaches into a bowl of boiling water for 30 seconds and carefully peel off and discard the blanched skins.

3

Halve the nectarines or peaches and remove and discard the stones. Chop the flesh and place in a blender or food processor with the kiwi fruit.

4

Remove the peel from the pineapple slices and cut into quarters. Cut away and discard the tough core from the pineapple and add the remaining flesh to the fruit in the blender or food processor.

5

Squeeze the juice from the lime and add to the fruit in the blender or food processor with the pineapple juice. Blend until smooth and pour into individual serving glasses.

6

Decorate the edge of the glasses with thin slices of unpeeled kiwi fruit or lime and serve.

Serving suggestions

Add some crushed ice just before serving if you like. Serve spooned over muesli for a refreshing breakfast.

Variations

Add 300 ml (½ pint) sugar-free lemonade to this recipe for a lighter, more refreshing fruit drink. Use unsweetened orange or apple juice in place of pineapple juice. Use 1 medium fresh mango in place of pineapple.

Cook's tip

Cover and chill the ingredients before serving, if you like.

Carrot Juice

Carrots and oranges are combined to produce a wonderfully vibrant-tasting drink.

Preparation time: 10 minutes • Serves: 2

Ingredients

300 g (10½ oz) carrots	*Salt and freshly ground black pepper*
½ red pepper	*Celery salt*
Juice of ½ lemon	*Sliced celery and leaves, to garnish*
Juice of 2 oranges	

Method

1
Scrape the carrots and set aside. Remove and discard the stalk, core and seeds from the pepper.

2
Chop the carrots and pepper into small pieces and purée in a blender or food processor until smooth.

3
Add the lemon and orange juices, then season with salt and pepper and celery salt to taste. Blend until well mixed.

4
Pour into glasses to serve and serve immediately, garnished with sliced celery and celery leaves.

Serving suggestion
Serve as a refreshing drink at breakfast time or any time during the day.

Variations
Use half carrots and half eating apples, peeled and cored, in place of all carrots. Use lime juice in place of lemon juice. Use pink grapefruit juice in place of orange juice.

Kiwi and Pineapple Shake

Sugar-free lemonade is easily available from supermarkets and adds a tangy fizz to this delicious fruity drink.

Preparation time: 10 minutes • Serves: 6

Ingredients

3 kiwi fruit	*Liquid sweetener, to taste*
225 ml (8 fl oz) pineapple juice	*425 ml (¾ pint) ice cubes*
1 lemon	*300 ml (½ pint) sugar-free lemonade*
300 ml (½ pint) low-fat plain yogurt	*1 kiwi fruit, for decoration*

Method

1

Carefully peel the 3 kiwi fruit and roughly chop the flesh. Place the kiwi flesh in a blender or food processor with the pineapple juice and blend until smooth.

2

Finely grate the rind from half the lemon and squeeze the juice. Mix the juice into the yogurt in a large jug with the fruit purée and liquid sweetener.

3

Place the ice cubes in the blender or food processor and pour over the pineapple and yogurt mixture. Blend for 15-30 seconds until it becomes a smooth slush.

4

Divide this mixture between 6 glasses and top up with lemonade, stirring well with a long-handled spoon to blend in the glasses.

5

Cut the unpeeled kiwi fruit into thin slices and slit each slice halfway through. Stand each slice of kiwi on the sides of each glass for decoration.

Serving suggestion

Serve with a light lunch or breakfast.

Variations

Use orange juice in place of pineapple juice. Use lime rind and juice in place of lemon. Use sugar-free orangeade in place of lemonade.

Cook's tip

Do not use set yogurt in this recipe, since it will not blend smoothly.

Yogurt with Carrot and Apple

This creamy fruit drink is ideal served for breakfast.

Preparation time: 10 minutes • Serves: 2-4

Ingredients

500 ml (18 fl oz) low-fat plain yogurt	*1 sharp-tasting eating apple*
Juice of 1 lemon	*2 carrots*
30 ml (2 tbsp) caster sugar	*Garden cress, to garnish (optional)*

Method

1

Place the yogurt, lemon juice and sugar in a bowl and mix well.

2

Peel and core the apple. Scrape 1 of the carrots. Grate both ingredients into the yogurt mixture and stir well to mix.

3

Pour into wide-brimmed glasses and sprinkle with garden cress if you like.

4

Scrape the remaining carrot, then cut into spirals using a canelling knife.
Use the spirals to garnish the drinks. Serve immediately.

Serving suggestion

Serve with toast or toasted muffins for a delicious breakfast.

Variations

Use a pear in place of the apple. Use lime or orange juice in place of lemon juice.
Garnish with fresh watercress sprigs in place of cress.

Almond-Yogurt Shake

This healthy, sugar-free yogurt shake has a slightly salty but refreshing flavour.

Preparation time: 10 minutes • Serves: 6

Ingredients

Salt	*1.25 ml (¼ tsp) saffron strands*
425 ml (¾ pint) low-fat plain yogurt	*10 ml (1 tsp) rosewater*
10 ml (2 tsp) lemon juice	*600 ml (1 pint) ice cubes*
30 ml (2 tbsp) ground almonds	

Method

1
Lightly moisten the rims of 6 tumblers with a little water. Spread a thin layer of salt onto a saucer and dip the moistened rims into the salt to coat lightly.

2
Place 200 ml (7 fl oz) water in a blender or food processor and add the yogurt, lemon juice, almonds, saffron and rosewater. Blend until smooth.

3
Mix in a further 200 ml (7 fl oz) water and salt to taste.

4
Pour the yogurt mixture from the blender or food processor into a large jug.

5
Place half the ice cubes in the blender or food processor and pour over half the yogurt mixture. Blend to a thick, smooth slush, then repeat with the remaining ice and yogurt mixture.

6
Pour into the prepared tumblers and serve.

Serving suggestion
Serve as an aperitif before a light lunch or supper, or serve at breakfast-time.

Variations
Use the juice of ½ orange in place of the lemon juice. Use ground hazelnuts in place of almonds. Add a few drops of almond essence in place of rosewater.

Strawberry Yogurt Ice

Ice cream made with low-fat plain yogurt and fresh fruit provides a welcome treat in a low-fat diet.

Preparation time: 15 minutes, plus freezing time • Serves: 4

Ingredients

225 g (8 oz) fresh strawberries	*1 egg white*
300 ml (½ pint) low-fat plain yogurt	*Liquid sweetener, to taste (optional)*
10 ml (2 tsp) powdered gelatin	*A few fresh strawberries, to decorate*

Method

1

Remove and discard the green stalks and leaves from the strawberries. Roughly chop the fruit.

2

Place the strawberries in a blender or food processor with the yogurt. Blend until smooth.

3

Sprinkle the gelatin over 30 ml (2 tbsp) boiling water in a small bowl. Stand the bowl in another bowl and pour in enough boiling water to come halfway up the sides of the dish.

4

Allow the gelatin to stand, without stirring, until it has dissolved and the liquid has cleared.

5

Pour the strawberry mixture into a bowl, then stir in the dissolved gelatin, mixing well to blend evenly. Pour the mixture into a shallow, freezerproof container and freeze until just icy around the edges.

6

Remove from the freezer, place in a chilled bowl and beat until the chilled mixture is smooth. Return to the container and freeze once again in the same way.

7

Remove from the freezer a second time, place in a chilled bowl and whisk with an electric mixer until smooth. In a separate bowl, whisk the egg white until it forms soft peaks.

8

Fold the whisked egg into the partially set strawberry mixture, carefully lifting and cutting the mixture to keep it light.

9

Sweeten with liquid sweetener to taste, if using, then return the strawberry ice to the container and return to the freezer to freeze until completely set.

10

Remove the yogurt ice from the freezer 20 minutes before serving to soften slightly. Scoop into serving dishes and decorate with a few extra strawberries.

Serving suggestion

Serve with sponge fingers or extra fresh fruit such as kiwi fruit and raspberries.

Variations

Use any other soft fruit in place of strawberries. It may be preferable to sieve blackcurrants or raspberries to remove the pips before adding to the yogurt as a purée. Use low-fat fruit-flavoured yogurt in place of plain yogurt.

Cook's tip

Use frozen or canned strawberries in place of fresh strawberries, but drain all the juice away first.

Fresh Fruit Platter

This inviting medley of fruit can be varied to suit your taste and availability of fresh ingredients.

Preparation time: 30 minutes, plus chilling time • Serves: 4

Ingredients

1 green fig	*1 medium mango*
2 kiwi fruit	*115 g (4 oz) seedless grapes*
2 fresh dates	*½ small melon*
1 guava	*225 g (8 oz) watermelon*
1 paw paw	*30 ml (2 tbsp) unsweetened orange juice*
115 g (4 oz) lychees	*30 ml (2 tbsp) lemon juice*
½ small pineapple	*25 g (1 oz) chopped walnuts or pine kernels (optional)*

Method

1
Select a large, shallow serving platter on which to arrange the fruit.

2
Cut the fig into quarters lengthways and arrange on the platter.

3
Peel the kiwi fruit and remove any hard core from the stem end. Thinly slice the fruit and arrange alongside the fig, reserving a few slices for the watermelon.

4
Cut the dates in half lengthways and remove and discard the stones. Add the dates to the serving platter.

5
Cut the guava in half and slice into wedges. Peel the paw paw and slice into thin crescents.
Arrange the guava and paw paw alternately on the platter with the other prepared fruit.

6
Peel the lychees and remove and discard the stones from the stalk end using the rounded tip of a swivel potato peeler. Place the fruit on the serving platter.

7
Peel the pineapple and cut away any brown eyes from the flesh. Cut the pineapple into slices and remove and discard the core using a sharp knife or an apple corer. Cut the pineapple into small wedges and arrange on the plate.

8
Peel the mango and cut the flesh into slices, discarding the stone. Halve the grapes and arrange the mango and grapes in an alternating pattern on the serving platter.

9
Peel the melon, cut in half and remove and discard the seeds. Slice the melon flesh into small wedges.

10
Leaving the peel and pips in place, cut the watermelon into small wedges. Arrange the melon and watermelon wedges on either side of the platter and decorate with the remaining kiwi fruit slices.

11
In a small bowl, mix together the orange juice, lemon juice and chopped nuts, if using, and drizzle over the fruit.
Cover with plastic wrap and chill well before serving.

Serving suggestions
Serve with low-fat yogurt ice, ice cream or plain yogurt.

Variations
Use chopped almonds, pecan nuts or hazelnuts in place of walnuts. Use apple or pineapple juice in place of orange juice.

Black Cherry Compote

Black cherries and apple juice combine perfectly in this flavourful low-fat dessert.

Preparation time: 15 minutes, plus chilling time • Serves: 6

Ingredients

675 g (1½ lb) fresh black cherries	*38 ml (2½ tsp) cornflour or arrowroot*
425 ml (¾ pint) unsweetened apple or grape juice	*45 ml (3 tbsp) brandy (optional)*
7.5 ml (1½ tsp) finely grated lemon rind	*Fresh mint sprigs, to decorate*

Method

1
Remove and discard the stones from the cherries using a cherry stoner or the rounded end of a potato peeler.

2
Place the cherries in a saucepan with the apple or grape juice and the lemon rind. Bring to the boil over a moderate heat, then reduce the heat and simmer for 10 minutes, or until the cherries are gently poached, stirring occasionally.

3
Remove the cherries from the juice with a slotted spoon, leaving the juice in the saucepan.
Arrange the cherries in a serving bowl.

4
In a small bowl, blend the cornflour or arrowroot with 75 ml (5 tbsp) of the cherry juice.

5
Add the blended cornflour or arrowroot to the cherry juice in the pan and bring to the boil, stirring continuously, until the sauce has thickened. Simmer for 2 minutes, stirring. Stir in the brandy if using.

6
Pour the thickened cherry sauce over the cherries in the bowl. Allow to cool, then chill well before serving.
Serve, decorated with fresh mint sprigs.

Serving suggestions
Serve with a dollop of low-fat ice cream, yogurt ice or low-fat yogurt.

Variations
Use fresh apricots in place of cherries. Use orange juice in place of apple or grape juice. Use sherry in place of brandy.
Use lime rind in place of lemon rind.

Pumpkin Seed Muffins

The aroma of freshly baked muffins is hard to beat, and these wholesome muffins
make an enjoyable dessert or snack.

Preparation time: 15 minutes • Cooking time: 30 minutes • Makes: 6-8

Ingredients

250 g (9 oz) cornmeal	*40 g (1½ oz) butter, melted*
7.5 ml (1½ tsp) baking powder	*5 ml (1 tsp) honey*
300 g (10½ oz) lukewarm low-fat plain yogurt	*2.5 ml (½ tsp) salt*
2 medium eggs, beaten	*50 g (1¾ oz) peeled pumpkin seeds*

Method

1
Mix the cornmeal and baking powder in a bowl.

2
Add the yogurt, eggs, butter, honey and salt and mix well until a smooth dough is formed.

3
Coarsely chop the pumpkin seeds and fold into the mixture.

4
Grease 6-8 muffin or bun tins and divide the mixture equally between them.

5
Bake in the centre of a preheated oven at 200°C/400°F/Gas Mark 6 for about 30 minutes, until risen and golden brown.

6
Transfer to a wire rack to cool. Serve warm or cold.

Serving suggestions
Serve on their own or with fresh fruit, or split and spread with a little low-fat spread, honey or reduced-sugar jam.

Variations
Use sunflower, sesame or poppy seeds in place of pumpkin seeds.
Use half white and half wholemeal flour in place of cornmeal.

Blackberry Fluff

Fresh blackberries have a wonderfully sharp, distinctive flavour – a taste to savour!

Preparation time: 20 minutes, plus chilling time • Serves: 4

Ingredients

450 g (1 lb) fresh blackberries	*Liquid sweetener, to taste*
300 ml (½ pint) plain low-fat set yogurt	*Whole blackberries and pieces of angelica, to decorate*
2 egg whites	

Method

1

Wash the blackberries thoroughly and place in a saucepan. Cover the pan with a tight-fitting lid and cook over a low heat for 5-10 minutes, stirring occasionally until the fruit softens. Remove from the heat and cool slightly.

2

Press the cooked blackberries through a nylon sieve using the back of a spoon to press out the juice and pulp. Discard the pips and reserve the purée.

3

Place the yogurt in a large bowl and beat in the blackberry purée until smooth and well mixed.

4

In a separate bowl, whisk the egg whites until they form very stiff peaks.

5

Fold into the blackberry purée without over-mixing the ingredients, to create an attractive marbled effect.

6

Sweeten with liquid sweetener to taste, then spoon into serving dishes and decorate with the whole blackberries and angelica pieces. Chill before serving.

Serving suggestions

Serve with sponge fingers or extra fresh fruit such as raspberries and strawberries.

Variations

Use raspberries or strawberries in place of blackberries. Use low-fat fruit-flavoured yogurt in place of plain yogurt.

Cook's tip

This recipe can be partially frozen to create a cooling summer dessert.

Apricots in Kefir

A quick and easy dessert, flavoured with kefir and honey.

Preparation time: 10 minutes, plus standing and chilling times • Serves: 4

Ingredients

4 large ripe apricots, weighing about 300 g (10½ oz) in total	*350 ml (12 fl oz) kefir*
20 ml (4 tsp) honey	*Fresh mint sprigs, to decorate*

Method

1
Prick the apricots all over. Place each apricot in a serving dish.

2
Place 5 ml (1 tsp) honey in each dish and divide the kefir equally between the dishes.

3
Cover and leave overnight at room temperature.

4
Chill for 1 hour before serving. Serve, decorated with fresh mint sprigs.

Serving suggestion
Serve with wafer biscuits.

Variations
Use small peaches or nectarines in place of apricots. Use maple syrup in place of honey.

Cook's tip
Kefir is a fermented liqueur traditionally made from camel's milk but now more commonly made from cow's milk.

Pears Helène with Quark

A luxurious, creamy dessert – ideal for summertime eating alfresco.

Preparation time: 10 minutes • Serves: 4

Ingredients

250 g (9 oz) quark (low-fat curd cheese)	*15 ml (1 tbsp) chocolate vermicelli or flakes*
100 ml (3½ fl oz) skimmed milk	*100 ml (3½ fl oz) unsweetened pear juice*
100 ml (3½ fl oz) soured cream	*Vanilla sugar, to taste*
4 canned pear halves, drained	*Chocolate leaves, to decorate*

Method

1
Place the quark, milk and soured cream in a bowl and mix together to form a creamy consistency.

2
Cut the pears into cubes and mix into the quark cream with the chocolate vermicelli or flakes and pear juice.

3
Add vanilla sugar to taste and mix well.

4
Spoon into dishes and serve, decorated with chocolate leaves.

Serving suggestions
Serve with sponge fingers or fresh fruit.

Mango Sorbet

This deliciously cool sorbet can be served either as a dessert or as a refresher between courses of a low-fat meal.

Preparation time: 15 minutes, plus freezing time • Serves: 4

Ingredients

3 mangoes	*1 egg white*
Juice of ½ lime	*Liquid sweetener, to taste (optional)*
125 ml (4 fl oz) dry white wine	*Fresh mint sprigs and mango slices, to decorate*
125 ml (4 fl oz) mineral water	

Method

1
Peel the mango and cut away the flesh from around the stone.

2
Place the mango flesh in a blender or food processor and blend until smooth.

3
In a bowl, mix together the puréed mango, lime juice, wine and mineral water.

4
Place the mango mixture in a shallow freezerproof container and freeze until just beginning to set around the edges.

5
Transfer to a chilled bowl and break up the ice crystals in the mango mixture using a fork, until smooth.

6
Whisk the egg white until stiff, then fold carefully and thoroughly into the mango mixture.
Sweeten with liquid sweetener to taste, if you like.

7
Return the mango mixture to the container and freeze until completely set.

8
To serve, remove from the freezer 20 minutes before serving, then scoop into individual serving dishes.

9
Serve, decorated with fresh mint sprigs and mango slices.

Serving suggestion
Serve with fresh fruit such as mixed berries or tropical fruit.

Variations
Use any other favourite fruit in place of mango such as strawberries or peaches. Use lemon juice in place of lime juice.
Use rosé wine or apple juice in place of white wine.

Index